Gallery Books
Editor Peter Fallon

A NEST ON THE WAVES

David Wheatley

A NEST
ON THE WAVES

David Wheatley

Gallery Books

A Nest on the Waves
is first published
simultaneously in paperback
and in a clothbound edition
on 14 October 2010.

The Gallery Press
Loughcrew
Oldcastle
County Meath
Ireland

www.gallerypress.com

*All rights reserved. For permission
to reprint or broadcast these poems,
write to The Gallery Press.*

© David Wheatley 2010

ISBN 978 1 85235 503 6 *paperback*
     978 1 85235 504 3 *clothbound*

A CIP catalogue record for this book
is available from the British Library.

Contents

for Aingeal

To Wilmington Swing Bridge

House on the swing bridge, house in the air,
standing aside for the barge from upriver,
let my dragging anchors not snag
on your cables while I confer
with my first mate, athwartships,
pondering our heading and draft.
The forecast promises shopping trolleys,
my lightermen poke at the muddy soup,
but I swim to the burger van and regain
my ship's cat's perch from terra non firma,
the forty-five degree angle of your
compliance to my chuntering purpose.

The dry bulk in the yards we pass
will be reduced to nothingness
and utility; my cargo exists
only in the subjunctive, yet not one
grain shall be lost. A lost swan
incubates a nest of golf balls
and a stray hand replaces the flowers
in the bridge-house window: red flowers.
House on a bridge, I hear the gears scream,
I feel each tooth of the terrible works
connect and, greased up, haul you back
to the fixity of empty air.

A Fret

The coal merchant shoulders a nimbus of smuts
down a street that insists you've been here before
and recognize the urchin — you — that sits
and stares at his shoes in an open front door.

Don't buy it. The air is thick with the sloughed
skin of dead selves: they fall and settle,
a load too imperceptible to shift,
but sickly and adhesive, mute and subtle.

Let them not expect grief. You dodge and move
through liquid fixities of past and present,
steer by a river whose mudbanks leave
you tidal, shifty, bogged down and imprisoned.

The sonic boom of the afternoon roar
from the stadium tracks your footsteps, blows
a dull wound in the boulevard's thin air,
and your pulse thuds to its drumbeat, win or lose.

On the up this year then? Play-off places,
blip, slump, plummet, dead in the water:
the mustard cuts like fog. Cut your losses,
a can kicked into the nearest gutter.

Here the last of empire has meandered
past the fag-end of the North Sea fleet
to a scrapyard sculpture park whose remaindered
Edward VII accepts a vain salute

from a yawning Ford Fiesta's bonnet.
The December sun is a lazy eye.
No vistas you can raise will open it
and you thirst for the liquid dark to bleed it dry,

and so comes evening and beer in a backstreet pub
by the bridge where you bank the coal fire down
and a dog sips a pint, and onto your tab
goes a Schlenkerla, the 'hobbling man';

and fog on the way home, fog all round
so I can't see you who are a shadow away,
and there are no shadows and there is no ground
underfoot for me to feel give way,

and what kind of weather is this when all I want,
all that I imagine, touch and see
finds, not loses, itself in all I cannot
grasp, in a fog drifted in from the sea?

On Tory Island

Starting from the end of the world —
a dead crab rattles its quayside pot
and my stomach declines the trip,
stays put on the pier
while its contents slosh
in a plastic bag. The wind stops
for a moment and we all fall down.

Given the painter's refusal
of perspective the island you are
bound for will now fall off
the edge of the sky. You are sailing
to and not from the mainland.
All islands are mainlands. This
is the world and all other corners its ends.

Knots of islanders stream from
the graveyard to East Town and West Town —
the infinite riches of if not one thing
the other — each soul one peg the more
to stop the place blowing away
with the trees (there are no trees
on the island), and the lighthouse beams,

blown out to sea and snapped at
by Balor's teeth where the island runs out.
Lighthouse beam, then dash,
dark, stop and wait: how it was
before streetlights, getting back
from the pub; beam, dash, dark, stop,
wait in the Atlantic-wide black-out.

The island disappears round me
in mist, the pier water is transparent
black. Believe with the harbour's

Tau cross in a faith long abandoned,
granting you nothing: miss the last boat
and look back on a cancelled world
through the one bleary eye in the back of your head.

In Glencolumbkille

Is fada ó bhaile a labhraíonn an pilibín.

It is far from its nest the lapwing sings.
Wherever it leads you you are misled
and where you look look elsewhere instead,
past the power lines' fiddle strings

fretted by thrush or dawdling chough
but not the lapwing, which keeps guard
far beyond the fingerboard
where the score, the notes and tune take off.

Never was absence of song more blessed
than in the ear of one who waits
seeking, then finding that not just its
but all silence here is a lapwing's nest.

On Mweelrea

I am climbing Mweelrea with my teeth.
The lightning of hunger flashes
from my blank eyes. One piece of grass
leads to another. Waves lead
the island of the bright cow to pasture
beyond Blacksod Bay. My twitching
ear to the ground takes what should be

its pulse, keener than glaciers,
deeper than fjords: the thunder is all
but audible. Days under wind
on a one-in-one slope I have you,
mountain, by your long grass root:
shake me off your back and you
will tumble into the sea and be lost.

A mountain with a sheep on its crown
is higher than any map allows,
but no foot passes my threshold
of cloud. I will reach the summit
and never have raised my eyes.
I will reach the summit and sink
gently into the roof of the sky.

Naiad

First find your wave
and breast it, break it.
Enter the weave
of the sea's pocket.

Leave the trail
of your heels' plunge
for the next swell
to rearrange.

Deliquesce
in your element.
Be past caress.
Be all I want.

The Antarctic Poetry School

Historically, the absence
of even one writer

has been the least
of the Antarctic School's worries.

Is its hallmark cool tone
sustainable in today's climate?

I suspect not, though
the Old Antarctic

for 'burning zeal' is 'thin ice,
beware' and 'splash, ha ha'.

Most traditional verse forms
are too complex to have been ever attempted.

Prizes are often awarded
but their recipients seldom informed.

Resentment of the more glamorous
South Georgia School runs high.

Annual poetry sales, it must
be said, never dip, not a unit.

Penguins are rarely mentioned
for fear of obviousness

though the albatross, where encountered,
is a symbol for penguins,

and the elephant seal
a symbol for the albatross.

The local note
is especially prized

on condition
that nobody strike it.

Another glacier
suicide

goes off to the most
wonderful splash.

Do you have this typeface
in white, please?

There is, between all
local dialects,

one word for snow
and that word is 'snow'.

E M Cioran in Tatters

I'd rather have been a plant, you bet,
and spent my life guarding a piece of shit.

*

All the philosophers combined
dissolve in the tears of just one saint.

*

Approach each day as a Rubicon,
not to cross but to jump in and drown.

*

My thoughts are only of God
since but for him I might
have to think about man instead
and could I sink lower than that?

*

Preposterous thought:
an impotent rat.

*

Epicurus, the sage I need most,
wrote three hundred books. Thank God they're all lost!

*

Not even a killer, I make no sense:
the Raskolnikov of innocence.

*

Will-to-die that I eat, sleep and breathe —
you've stolen it from me, stolen my death.

*

No sleep as tight
after decades without
as the sleep of the man
they'll shoot at dawn.

*

Who more than I has embraced his fate?
At birth I was offered the world on a plate
and screamed at them, Sorry, too late, too late!

Girl on the No 13 Bus

after Max Jacob

O majorette, flexible friend,
leggy lass, O legs without end!
legging it at half past nine
for the bus from Orchard Park to town.
Don't you miss out, girl, I ask you,
on the ride now pulling out of Tesco.
Your swelling heart does karaoke
to its own beats for getting lucky,
and off you speed into the night
that pulses to the Humber's tide;
and though I'm not about to wallow
I've longed too long already, willow.
People of Drypool, Drypool folk!
promise me someone gives a fuck.
Bus-stop queues, go whistle Dixie,
wait for the next one or get a taxi.
When next you see her flick her mane
she'll have crossed the finishing line
with the yellow jersey on her chest
to join the boy that she loves best,
her toyboy and our bouncing kid.
She may live here but she comes from Brid.
This girl don't go off on one neither.
Look at those lips. That's why I bother.

Sweat

Saline meniscus we secrete
as our limbs wrap, knit and attune,
our rough drafts left behind on the sheet:
sealing by stretching the space between
my flank and your flank, my chest and yours,
the extra space of a liquid pinch
that comes away in our hands and pours
us out of each other, the mingled drench

we tip out through the tips of our tongues
and down the gutters of palms and spine;
the pool of us gathered by shoulders and hips
we each collect, that insists as it clings
I am your outside now and you mine:
the sweat we lick from and leave on our lips.

Semaphore

A ship in a bottle, a ship in a bulb.
My love the lighthouse-keeper sleeps
in a circular bed, his toes almost

touching his head, and I his wife
dance by the shore, a flag in each hand.
He watches me from inside the storm

and knows the code. Red,
yellow, red: I found your toothbrush,
the swallows have fledged. The light

has a god's all-powerful whimsy —
flashing, occulting, isophase —
and he's the man will catch fish with a kite,

and knit me a chough's red beak
on a jumper. Come the worst
of the swells relief is impossible:

where is the light to warn the man
inside the light and under the sea's
own tongue? When they saw

the Flannans lamp dark and no one
to greet them the search party
knew the island unmanned,

its savage tideline notional
henceforth, up in the air.
I too am carried away

who have gone nowhere.
But, oh, he's the man will come
back to me, winched over

the waves with his jigsaws done
to a total absence of potted meat,
to where no spray leeches into our bed.

Little Ones

DEDICATION

It's all yours.

THREAD

Wing-mirror spider
    sitting tight
        all motorway long

        takes my finger,
    come journey's end
cuts loose and moves on.

POUND SHOP

That its value for money
not falter or fail

opens for business
with a closing-down sale.

SWIMMING

I ploughed a field forty times
        nothing grew
as I gave up
        it sprouted
                me.

LOUGH DAN UNREACHED

Not that the path was lost
but that after long
hesitation the briars
had found and embraced it at last.

DERELICT HOUSE

Though I bricked myself in
and still nobody came

I'll stand here and wait
for you just the same.

HALL OF MIRRORS

The closer I get to myself the more I shrink.
You loom larger and larger walking away.

Triskets

At the Sign of the Empire that Came and Went,
at the Sign of the Fudge-coloured Cat,
we are well met. There is time
between the waiter's leisurely rounds

for the currency to change and change back.
The Futurist Volunteer Bicycle Brigade.
Caporetto. *M'illumino d'immenso.*
The old Austrian statues going back up

here, now, but under what flag?
The end of war need not be defeat
but obscurity raised to a fine art.

Another empire could come and go
and the beer at this café still be flat.

(Trieste)

*

O my Slovenia, fanatically mild
and unknown! Empire's glove-compartment,
land of modestly-priced swimwear and cheese,
and the capital with the loveliest name.

I fancied the hills full of knee-high bears.
Walking among vineyards I found a toy
scorpion pricking the air above its head,
defying you and your army's ignorant boot heels

and taking for victory the nearest gap,
reversible-into, in the drystone wall.
The bells peeled on the hour in honour

of Our Lady of the Tape Recorder.
There was no bell-ringer. There were no bells.

The Cormorant

I love the cormorant's impetuous thrust
into green water that variegates to rust
from his assault, that sensual terrorist.
I love your sweat-beads' tryst

with the back of your neck and the line they traced
over your ribs as we undressed
to swim. I take the current on trust.
I am any old ignorant tourist.

Put this afternoon down as the driest
on record if the thunder holds off, but first
translate this mood of mine from triste

here where one tongue washes another, reversed
around the other's saline edge of thirst.

Gurgles

Round here it's real and it matters. All my life I've wanted to come here, behind the sorting office on the industrial estate, and stand on this corner, blinking. Round here it hurts. Name a gland and that's where the pain is, bending you double or leaving you numb: either will do, neither will do. Here a man can grow old among the allotments and give thanks, or freeze over slowly, cursing himself, as the preference takes him. When I consider the horrors of life back at home, the patina of dust closing my eyelids, I wish that I'd stayed there. Then when I think of the good things I'm glad that I came, glad I escaped them. I'm funny like that. I used to hang from the strap as the train emerged from the tunnel and look for the island out in the bay, the whitewashed jetty, the tower and the church — oh every time, most times, sometimes, never, delete as applicable. Trailing my hand in the water on the boat ride and hiding the sunlight I trapped in my pocket — I have it there still. Miss the last boat, secrete yourself among the rabbit warrens and goat droppings and be again among the druid remains: plague refugee, king of Dalkey, duke of Muglins and sovereign of the illustrious order of the lobster and periwinkle. The island is a Cyclops, a Cyclops called Noman, Noman is an island, the tower is his eye, *omen est nomen, omen est Noman*, and far from losing his one good eye the maimed Cyclops will grow a second, and quite a view he'll have from it too. Of it all, of the whole shebang. Dad wants to climb Killiney Hill again for our Sunday excursion: that must be him you see on the summit, piling up stones, one on top of the other, and waving. Tell him you're busy but expect to be home by teatime. It'll probably be what, corned beef and cabbage, my favourite. The jellyfish dance in formation, the skeletal pirates shake in their cages on the outlying rocks and teatime finds you flat on your back in the gorse, with maybe a goat licking your face or chewing your beard, the bashi-bazouk. I never did like my favourite much anyway, truth be told. I trot round the corner to the sorting office and slide my apology under the door.

The Recusant

Sans mal désir

I have persisted in the old faith.
A chimney-pot pigeon sits
like a hen on the rumble of prayer
from the priest hole below.
Let the fox in the long grass go home
hungry if only this egg might hatch.

Do not call the house empty.
The seigneur has not departed
but vanished, the better to linger
unnoticed. An attendant runs
a duster over the words
'deodand', 'escheat' and 'estray'.

A sea-turtle shell, a sawfish snout:
the sea is a grave and my cabinets
are the sea's own grave. My prize
whale rose to his fall: along
his spine's whispering gallery
echoes of his death roar carry and break.

About m'lady's silver powder
hangs a whiff of vinegared lead.
A frolicking Cupid smiles through
a marble scarf frayed to transparency
and asphyxiates slowly; Ariadne
is carried away on a panther's back.

A playbill reads *In Preparation,*
The burlesque of the ratcatcher's
daughter. A scurry of feet
on the back stairs announces if not

the daughter the catcher, if not him
the rats. They have my applause.

Before they depart my last artist
and model will fill the one space left
on the library wall. One day you
will feast on her breast and know beauty.
I shall call it 'English School
(17th century, sitter unknown)'.

(Burton Constable Hall)

At the Sign of Ye Olde White Harte

Every man can dig water at his door; and they cannot bury a corpse
there but the grave first drowns him ere it burys him.
                                    — *The Life of Master John Shawe*

Dead men in a city besieged,
your own graves would harry you out.
The pavement eel's stone slither
along the old town's dark intestine
shows where they follow
their shadows to spawn. One
passageway leads to another,
one courtyard swallows another,
until all passageways are one
and every dead end turns
like a folded paper trick
inside out. Do not expect spice
from the Land of Green Ginger,
though there is powder aplenty.
A sworn rite governs our fellowship
and only my skull in a box besides
be privy: the pot-boy crouched
by the smallest window in England
awaits but the signal. Small
acts of sedition multiply:
chalk marks on the pavement
cry death and the misericord
under your bottom has started
to flap in the breeze. The city
gates stay shut, let his Majestie
make of this what he maye;
the skull has spoken. The shadows
spawn and crawl into the dark
to die. *How you have bled*
for me, o my Kingdome.
The Land of Green Ginger

turns itself inside out
to a dream of green fields:
*yet may we attain to that place
of peace in our hearts.* There is
no way out and we leave tonight.

Migrant Workers

If there are dozens there are a hundred,
frost on their boots but some bare-chested.
Not one green shoot will be wasted:
migrant workers, drifters, kindred

come from towns out east to stoop
to the earth this harsh-grained Lincoln dawn,
then stretch by the road, their day's shift done,
stopping when this man says they stop.

This one has a Master's degree,
this one a girl in Brno and
a girl in Grimsby. His best friend
will kill a third in some skulduggery.

Some will not know, how you say,
names for what they pick in English,
for pleasure, tedium or anguish,
for banks of poppy, wild rose, daisy.

Next summer finds them here or gone
as the market or their whims dictate.
The children they have yet to meet
call here/there home in this/that tongue.

Despair

after Seán Ó Ríordáin

No dead men will leave the tomb
to seek out the confines of night or day.
Abandon your designs on them
and humble your bare head to the clay.

Don't think you can put flesh on a wraith.
The beautiful was never true.
I know that My Redeemer lieth.
No pennies will fall from heaven for you.

You want a pooka to breathe down your neck,
and all the heavenly lies he'd spin.
You've settled for the hump on your back:
don't let it spread to the brain.

Amidst your pooka shadowmancy
find the pooka truth and way.
Cast a hunchshadow all can see
and humble your bare head to the clay.

Make a show of yourself. The critic rates
the hunchshadowself you hide in
that once was laid between the sheets
to kiss while deafness blew from heaven.

And a gentle hand entombed and rotting,
a dream in a separate tomb imprisoned,
the dearest dream, the rarest thing,
in a deep tomb inside the mind,

and the black chalice of night drained low,
and a crooked sleep, tossed left and right,
while Veronica mopped His brow,
while the hunchback stripped bare in the night.

Hypocrite lecteur who read
the poem I beget on sickness,
try judging *that* and then decide
what is failure and what success.

Two Saints

In fact, there is only God and me.
— E M Cioran, *Tears and Saints*

Catherine never saw
without wanting to kiss

a leper's sore,
she whose flesh

throve on something
so like fresh air

(body of Christ),
any more

was already as much
as she could bear.

To the pure in heart
all is pure.

We are not ourselves.
We are His vessels.

The dead saint's head
the faithful sever

turns to a bagful
of rose petals.

I the leper am healed
of my evil.

Now heal me as fast
of your cure.

(*Catherine of Siena*)

*

If the heart is game
Christ is its hunter.

In your name, Francis,
the wolf is my brother.

In the name of the wolf,
the dogs and the birds

named in your prayers,
all living things

we place in your care;
except the wolf

I can endure,
but your perfection

is too much to bear.
It is Christ the hunter,

gentle Francis,
who bites and who tears.

At the close of your life
your near-blind eyes

were found to be sealed
by a lifetime of tears.

(*Francis of Assisi*)

Jack Yeats, 'The Barrel Man'

How easy people must be to please
when even brickbats count as applause.

It takes a peace-loving man indeed
to brave such war and not lose his head.

Today's Diogenes must learn
to ride the rapids in his urn

but no Niagara plunge compares
to testing the waters above my ears.

What's a ducking to one fed on
the kind of weather I bang my head on?

I am the dung-heap where the fruit
you plant on me will lodge and sprout,

my rotten-tomatoed two black eyes
the sick-note for my clown's disguise.

The windfalls in this antic zoo
mean not just fruit but the branches too:

I am your tuppenny Christ expected
to salvage his own cross from your dead wood.

If a baying crowd pelts with ardour
an appreciative one just pelts the harder.

Grant me, O Lord, a knockout blow
and over I'll roll and off I'll go.

In Memory of the N11

Site of the next smash
victim's roadside shrine,
who and wherever: waiting,

sped past. The Sugarloaf's
shark-fin tip overhead,
sniffing blood.

Tarmac in my veins
but not once underfoot,
how you burn for me,

shimmer and burn.
The inside lane peels off
for the garden centre

and the driver turns
the radio up for the sport.
The road has eaten

a small village
under the sign of
its service station's

knife and fork;
we drive through
someone's front room.

A child in a hillside field
flies a kite, and a cat
one lane from the road

is asleep in the sun.
Stream through my eyes,
kite girl, their shade

to your light. On still
evenings the fox's cry
at the end of your lane

must carry all the way
to the flyover. It wipes
its nostrils clean of my scent.

The minute underground throb
of the bus's passing shakes
my grandparents' bones.

Rush hour, sometimes,
a body can feel it's never
going to move.

Towns are concessions,
begrudged. Dip in the road
where a bloodline

rose, sank, settled,
'D'ye know what I'm goin'
to tell ye,' a generation's

worth of opening
conversational gambit
at the Village Inn,

Uncle Joe. Roads
without traffic
after the upgrade

don't go untravelled,
merely become
their own destination.

Figure looming
smaller and smaller
on the hospital drive

staring me full
in the back as I scarcely
glance up from my paper:

not until you are out
of sight do I think
to look, then a left,

and another pocket
handkerchief graveyard,
and that was a great day

for the village, the green
and red football flags
by the Marian grotto

will say, meaning
that not-to-be-forgotten
triumph, meaning that never-

again-to-be-mentioned
disgrace. The misspelled
takeaway sign awaits

the last drunks
and the king of the pipers
lies under a snowstorm

of flecked marble chips
but snow is not general.
There is no snow,

is only an evening
coming down, with
from the far docks

the sound of a foghorn
while the Sugarloaf slips
behind its veil to digest

the day's catch. You sit
in a blunted pencil of light
and a current of recycled air,

but don't imagine
there's no arriving, no
retiring you into

the slipstream with scarcely
a backward glance
from the driver. Your seat

is only so comfortable
and only the road
has no home to go to,

the one true static thing.
A last boy leaves
the misting-up windscreen

empty before you,
stepping off
at the edge of town,

its moving blackout
a pleasure deferred
long enough.

Now on your way
with you! It is two hours
ago again but

do not run
for the last bus:
you are on it and gone,

waving not me
but the bus stop
goodnight and already

hearing the foghorns
to greet you.
Goodnight.

The Shadow Life

for Raymond Magee

I would have been at the garden centre
on some deathly Sunday outing
and you at the rifle range a saunter
away in uniform sharp-shooting,

blind to the thought of your parents' house
a few fields down, say, one crack shot,
but further off than Congo or Cyprus
and reachable by no known route.

I would have been on the Belfast train
and missed you by no more than decades
when you took your Northern turn,
on the first of two one-way tickets —

Dublin-Belfast-Dublin again,
doubled back but to no return
to, not a home, but a place found gone,
a town of roots unbound and thrawn.

(Home, if we must say home, being what
but a word we use.) You and your brother,
that stranger, might have swapped his commute
to Tallaght, all that ring-road bother,

and your outings to Bray promenade
and up Bray Head, through all those years,
and swapped but still not met the need
for the other life: not his or yours,

but both, neither, all through the 40s,
60s, 80s, when you were, Dad

was, I was . . . when we crossed on forays
to and from Dublin, on the road

to Tallaght, to Bray, and overlapped
in ignorance, in strangeness shared,
but mutely as the pulse that throbbed,
then hammered, turning into the yard

of a Templeogue pub this spring, where you,
somebody's uncle, brother, son,
sipped a coffee, and that was our shadow
life, here and this one all along:

all the years' false trails unspooled;
lost and found, wrong our whole lives,
but returned to ourselves, grateful, appalled
how the road decides where the road home leads.

Flotsam

A cormorant drying its wings
steps down refreshed from its cross.
The sliver of moon is an ill-fitting
lid on the jar of our night
and the darkened lighthouse
has long been in league with the rocks.
A laughably happy small dog

fetching a stick no one has thrown
redoubles my prints in the sand,
kicks through and erases them.
I will not sail. Cover all
my traces as effortlessly
and I will stay for the last train,
the last boat to sail, and beyond.

Trailer Park Ghost

Brad Mehldau, you were
born a week after me

and have spent a lifetime
overcompensating.

Your albums come in so fast
that buying the new one

I sometimes get the unrecorded
one after that by mistake,

and am glad. Is it time
to bid farewell forever

again to the past with another
suavely whispering standard?

Goodbye storyteller, sings
a wispy line three octaves up,

meaning, once more
round the contraflow,

my rakish chromatic uncle:
a remembered condom of fluff

on a needle, an umbrella hat
permanently expecting rain.

A trailer park ghost
dodges bass-lines in 7/8 time.

I've heard some rueful whistling
in strange hotels, but only you

have chased leaves round the porch
in all the places I've never been.

This venue not on the T-shirt.
There is no T-shirt.

Against what modulations,
what untold fallings away,

should I steel myself,
remembered as they happen,

heard through arpeggio drizzle
and tipped from a lazy weekend's

shopping, the door key passed
greedily over the shrink wrap?

Too late the left hand sees
the turn off the freeway:

no bridge passage now
till New Jersey and no one but me

in the car to sing along.

La Ultima Canción de César Peru

I sought you by night
when the screech owl roared,

when, grave as a newborn child,
impulsive as a dying man,

the triplets on the beggar's guitar
sputtered like tachycardia.

Far to the west
guano archipelagos

fall sheer away
to the breakers, but how

much heavier than one
are two shadows thrown

on the same cobbled square,
draping the admiral's statue

here in our landlocked state.
You draw the curtains

and Inti the sun god
disperses his relics among

the pedlars' trinkets
that his mysteries

might hide in plain view,
lurk amid joyous vulgarity

above all suspicion. And so
it is with our sacred things,

parcelled out among conversations
with the road sweeper and milkmaid,

eccentrically calm
as a telephone call

taken during sex.
The oxygen thins out,

the faces in each street
redder than the last

until we scarcely remember
what saint's day we celebrate,

pushing aside a dovecote
of penitents' flapping white hoods

as we pick through
the washing lines on the tight

hillside streets. House
after house the doors grow

smaller, sharp-eyed
women stooping

and squinting as I salute, until
I enter the house of my childhood

down on all fours. Immortal
forgetfulness, immortal

misrecognition, I remember
and know you too well,

with always the kettle come
to the boil as I enter the door.

When will I learn
to roar like the screech owl?

When you stoop
to my window, dark one,

rattle my walls and bid me
follow somewhere only

this chosen, narrowest
entrance could lead.

Caravanserai

The Sahara has shifted
an inch and a continent.

The dune you are standing on,
Ibrahim Ag Alhabib,

is also thousands of miles
from your feet: my windscreen

this morning is coated
in fine desert sand.

Never was shifty heart truer,
or truer to it its far-scattered sons

who touch across oceans of sand.
Among themselves

the Touareg are the Imazighen,
'the free people'. In Arabic

'Touareg' means 'forsaken by God'.
The sandmen of my youth

are forsaken by the Fassaroe pit,
the last gravel mixed

and the compacted fill
rolled flat. I see again

the brace of wheels
on the weighbridge, the great

engines ticking over,
at bay, and dust

that is no longer sand
in the drivers' eyes.

I feel its drift, voiceless
and huge, within me,

and know I too
am transported, grain

by grain, and unsigned for,
the docket still in my father's hand.

Over that brutalized earth
I see the tippers void

the rising clouds of their sandstorms,
a caravanserai

of transients negotiate
sand trails decades since

the sand was there:
their mounts departed,

not a Thermos between them,
they and their shallow pits

soon exhausted, tiny-seeming
under the stars.

Lament for Ali Farka Touré

Hippo, baby hippo,
at the waterhole

where the crocodile's
narrowed eyes stare

from the pool,
O thirsty hippo,

what will you do?

          *

A child beating a hubcap hung
from a branch is the signal

the Arma has come. He rides
with the praise-singing griots

who play the ngoni and chant:
'Banzoumana is a great man.

He has left nothing shameful
behind him. His glory

will live on,' they chant,
and the desert wind

confiscates even his name.

          *

When the child spies a snake
at the edge of the fields

the spirits attack.
Bind him, take him away!

'What is that tune
you are playing, djinn?'

Bassekou sings. 'I am
a griot and you must tell me.'

'I call it *Ba La Bolo*,'
the djinn answers,

'*The Branch of the River.*'
For a year the boy and the spirits

do battle. He returns
with a tune on his lips:

all praise to Jimbala!
Ancestral and river spirits,

Pepsi and Sicilian-style spirits
join us this evening

where Bassekou sings
Ba La Bolo in Chez Thierry

and we dine on the best
pizza in Bamako.

*

The Manding empire,
the Songhai empire.

Colonial wars, tribal wars.
Nomad uprisings,

desertification. Abandonment
of migration routes

and slaughter of livestock.
The flight to the camps

and the blue of the Touareg,
the blue people's robes

(the men alone veiled,
the women riding bareheaded

behind them) disappearing
over the sand dunes

like a last trickle of water
at an emptying pool,

with nowhere in sight
to plug in his electric guitar

that Ibrahim wears
over his shoulder.

＊

The leper
beats his stumps

arhythmically
on the djembe drum,

then offers it to you,
its skittish goatskin

footsteps retreating,
fainter and fainter,

until your hands stop.

        *

The Dogon dancers celebrate
Sirius, the binary star,

see the moons of Jupiter
with their bare eyes.

Stilt dancers imitate
the long-legged waterbirds

and the priest points
to *po tolo*, the heaviest star

but 'the smallest thing there is'.
The melanin theory,

the astronaut theory:
untrue. Reject them.

Traders' tales:
we tell you these things

and you tell them back.
The masks discarded

after the dance
haggle with us

over the price
of a rich, hollow laugh.

*

This belongs in no book.
If found in a book

consider it lost
and return to its keeper.

A ball of clay hurled into space
by the god Amma is earth.

It is shaped like a woman.
It has for clitoris

a termite mound
which Amma removes

to couple with it.
She gives birth to a jackal

and half-human, half-
serpentine children:

the lords of the universe.
Seeing their mother's

nakedness they fashion
a skirt: language.

Their speechless, in-
subordinate brother,

Pale Fox, sees,
is jealous, and couples

with her. Thence
comes evil. Pale Fox

is possessed
of the gift of divination.

Sniffing round
the Hogon priest's throne

this morning in search
of his mother he sees

a line of ants
delicately negotiate

a gleaming knife's edge,
then slinks away leaving

a whiff of urine and
(this can't be right) menses.

＊

Look for me inside the
upside-down baobab tree.

It is I live there now,
underground, my shed

skin hung in flitches to cure
and my head buried in shame.

Sit in my shade and eat kola nuts
while I covet your spittle.

You are well punished,
the god declared, inverting

to humble the tree
that walked. My roots

in the air are a nest
of blind snakes,

but they see you,
see you and watch.

*

The line of sweat on Toumani
the kora master's fingers

is the watering hole
where tune after tune

comes to drink.

*

In my tongue Mali
means 'hippo' and Bamako

'place of crocodiles'.
The hippo and crocodile

steep side by side
in the pool, the mud

in- and exhaling their stillness,
with only their eyes

and pricked ears
for the vigil of hunger

and fear to perch on
and not deliciously drown.

       *

The river rises, sun-baked
and hardened, to give thanks

for itself in the mud
mosque sweating under

its ostrich-egg caps
and awaiting the women

to come sponge it down.
A goat's capsized reflection

shakes a silent bell
under the tide that rocks

the pirogue. We bring
you millet and salt

from the outlying villages
and desert mines.

What do you offer us
in return? The proud

Fulani girl sits in the bow
spurning your cowrie shells

and will not marry you
this year or next. Do not

look to the sky for the sun:
I think we are inside it.

The washerwomen on the banks
of the Niger empty

from their calabashes
tongues of laughing,

cooling fire.

*

Monsieur le Maire de Niafunké
returns from the well at sunset

with the walk of a trader
after the fair, whistling

a tune whose name
means happiness

and slapping the rump
of the first donkey he passes.

*

Our humpbacked caravan
halts precisely

nowhere and the bud
of the camel's head sinks

on its pendulous stalk
to the sand, her belly full

of nourishing thorns.
I loosen my boots

and the scorpion stirs
in a faraway dune:

we will have much
to catch up on, he and I!

River traders, it was
with the river, not you,

that I traded: I emptied
my gourd into the mud

in return for the Tamashek
words for 'water is life',

and sang with you, djinn:
'First son who has never been matched,

thank you for what never ends, yes!'

Curlew by the Humber

Hooped over turned earth
they stalk between tides,
unlooked for but found,
approaching.

The stubble of worms
they take shaved clean
at the root, loose grass
on the breeze

                    and shifting
temporary islands somewhere
behind the high ditch
world enough for them —

held
in a gaze
they do not return
tracking their looped cries

upwards and peeling
away as one at last
that I might know
what I have seen.

For the Night Parrot: Australia

JETLAG

I swapped the northern for the southern ocean.
I gained and lost time, cheating it like Oisín.
Up was down. Clarity was confusion.
The words I spoke had suffered an inversion.
The brilliant light of dawn was grey and ashen.

GREEN, ORANGE, RED

His song is goodbye, even
as he chirps hello
from his dead-wood hollow,

the orange-bellied parrot
chirping his gay old sorrow.

He has swallowed his halo:
it glows, a traffic light
suggesting an imminent stop.

In the event of a crash
remember to clean up

these twigs and seeds, and pin
to my breast an orange letter
reading O for zero.

FOR THE NIGHT PARROT

Flyover, sleepover timezones, daylight
saved and squandered. A Norfolk pine at dusk

screaming with hundreds of rainbow lorikeets.
When landfall comes it comes on a thermal

of rain, warm rain. Zygodactylous,
I walk forwards and backwards at once,
line my casuarina, my creaking hollow,
with gum-leaves and enter tail first.

I drink your health in mangrove and dead-wood pollen
and strip the bark to cheeky, fluttering tongues.
Wattle and eucalypt leaves are also acceptable.
I will preen as I feed you, smoothing your feathers,

their lattice-work of barbules and hooks cresting
to flares of sulphurous delight and alarm.
Out of the seeds we blossom and fledge, an irruption,
the pine dispersing to fill the whole morning sky.

I have begun to speak with the voice of a bird.
Whose voice, warbling, booming, falsetto,
will I imitate if not my own? I perch
on my own shoulder and whisper into my ear.

'Hey there!' chatters my particular friend
the gang-gang but having got my attention
deems all further need for speech at an end;
stonewalls my polite enquiries, preferring

to dip, bob and stare straight ahead.
The more I display the more stays hidden,
visible only in UV, my coverts an open
secret by now. Which leaves the night parrot:

to be spoken of in the is/was tense, this artist's
impression done from an artist's impression.

Its one-way tunnels have penetrated
all the way into the earth and not come back:

a roadside carcass, 1990, first
in a hundred years and the last. One partial
PS, 2006, found headless:
Orpheus of the night parrot's vanishing

act, the head rolling and whistling its way
to a halt in a dry river bed; the Maenads
cheated of their triumph, keening and comfort-
less among the spinifex ever since.

FOR THE FLYING FOX

How long have you been hanging over my head?
You scavenge on daylight and swallow it up
as you fly. Teardrops of darkness lingering
in the fig-tree branches ripen slowly

and drop: everywhere is a casual patience
of black awaiting the dark within dark
of flying blind, at large among the over-ripe
figs where the night will come away in your hand.

Mother-infant knot, you look fore and aft
as you go and, greedy, find your foliage
by crash's law. Surprise yourself with a hindfoot
snatch of fruit you right, very wrongly right

yourself to swallow. I've heard all the tales:
darkness reigned and the bat sent a boomerang
round the world in search of the vanished light —
but this is your story, why am I telling your story,

well you might ask in furious ultrasound,
your hearing too fine to abide the oafish
wavelengths I haunt. Optic nerve, fig-tree
perch, equator: three times my image

on your retina has been inverted;
three times over correct before you cancel
my image folding back into itself
the narrative on bat's wing leather I traced

and abandoned as you took wing: the bat
saved daylight and was most graciously thanked.
Humanity was nowhere. I slept through it all.
Your tight black cape falls from my shoulders

and my head spins, dangled slipping from the black
point of your talon piercing a fig. Night-blind
now I stare at what might be hundreds of bats
or none, here, there, everywhere, nowhere.

TASMANIA

My far-flung route held neither silk nor spice.
Beyond the reach of turnkeys, trackers, spies,
I swapped my chains for the jail of infinite space.
I gave my natives a blanket and bottle apiece.
Devils scream me to sleep. I sleep in peace.

Exequy

Not to endure like a needy old man,
ears full of hair and shouting

at the bare-chested boys
to get off your lawn.

Not to hang on like the wheezing
old woman who proves

such an annoyance clambering
onto the bus. To die

as you've lived,
a yellow-bellied dog,

stomach full of sawdust and scraps,
between the security fence

and the flyover, thoughtfully,
out of harm's way.

The Lock-keeper's Daughter

Take me away from this terrible place,
very slowly, by barge, rising through
the frothy lock outside my window
like an old cinema organ.
Ours will have been the most tacit
of courtships, the most offhand
of consummations as I step
aboard from the vegetable patch.
Expressionless townsfolk will process
from the church to the water's edge
and my discarded bouquet float by
to the wheeze of an accordeon waltz.
I too have dreamed of a tattooed
first mate and an infestation
of cats in the saucepans and hold.
The candour of my wedding dress
will face down scarecrows
and cornfields from the prow.
Take me away from this terrible place
two or three miles down the water,
no more: nowhere else can I
be happy but where the water voles
splash and the kingfisher combusts.
I hear the lock close behind me
and grant the water its steely
abolition of our having
ever passed through. I will walk
the length of the barge backwards
to you and into our future.

St Brenhilda on Sula Sgeir

My brother St Ronan gave me
the first fulmar of spring, but when
he praised my legs as I prayed

something screamed louder
than a storm beach of seals,
touched closer than the snugness

of a bed among rocks. I would not
have it: set sail, becoming
the flat earth's edge, living on guga

and cress, telling my prayers
by the light of a cormorant lamp,
its pentecostal tongue

its own wick. In its oily glare
nothing is illuminated.
Shall I preach to the birds?

I have seen the fork-tailed petrels
walk on water. It is no wonder
the miracle would be to see them

walk on land: a dozen yards
from shore they are wrecks,
lost for want of the ground

giving way. What, if I preach
to the birds, should I promise them
more than they have? The petrels

nest on the waves, an egg
under each wing. Fall
and ascend. I go down

easy into the earth, rise
again to the wispy tuft
of a shag's nest under

my picked-clean ribs.

In Valleymount

I hear the hammers
    tap a pulse
        from the veins of granite:

the stonecutters
    have returned
        from New Mexico,

their landfall a washout
    where the waters lie
        still over

the drowned
    reservoir townlands.
        What scanter

December light
    could I watch us by,
        how blinder a sun,

lining up
    the rifle sight
        of the passage grave

above the hill,
    its midwinter dust
        that much less

in the dark than I?
    But in Valleymount Church
        we are reconciled

by the blue glass
    of the Virgin's blouse
        to the gloom besides:

I have brought her
        least of all faith
                her crown's

topaz and ruby
        barnacled
                to the black

and unavailing
        against it.
                Stained glass

is water moving
        too slowly to catch,
                Proteus

in glacial time
        leaving us
                for dead:

I have brought her
        a candle
                that will drown too

before the evening
        is out
                as the ghost

of a hammer
        passes clean
                through the glass;

its light is what
        we see the dark by
                and it is blinding.

At Sally Gap

The placeless place:
find it incline
to the back roads'

slant invitation,
a colour code
rainbow away

on the map —
primary secondary
third class

other — the signs
in neither kilo-
metres nor miles

the Irish spelling
a qualm of variants
snagged on

a barbed-wire fence
through which
incurious

lours a sheep's
colour-of-ditch-
water face

this long-ago
Sunday after-
mass drive

revisited;
the gearbox
consumptive

the windscreen
in tears, and who
remains

for the Redcoats
to chase laying
the Military Road

as they go
and their heads
on their barracks'

stone pillows
the misspelt
patriot the lost

German soldiers
memorialized
out of memory

here where God
becomes Featherbed
Mountain

the monstrous
pylons striding
ahead and sunk

in the infant
Liffey's
breaking waters;

turf-cutter
tramper and twitcher
dodging

the heather spikes
on the sheep trails
and sparing

a glance as we pass
the corrie's
inverted dunce-

cap plumbing
the lacustrine
depths;

and if there were
houses there are
no houses

the rundown
national school
and struggling pub

cease to be
of concern where
the joyriders

burn out their cars
and walk home
and the radio mast

tears open
the sky on a sinkhole
draining

upwards and out
of everywhere
from the overrun

seaboard the hereby
declared abolished
city beyond

the helplessly
fertile midlands
and upstart

bustle of derelict
Glendalough:
we rise

without trace
the any-day-now
impassable roads

all too open
to your forecast
of issueless

whiteout
that does not come
but have we not

been here before
pulling over
might I not

merely
for once delight
in the sheep droppings

the beer cans
and facing four ways
choose all or none

knowing well
dusk will find us
at sea-

level the mountains
stacked
asleep again

behind the last
estate's teatime
lights, all that

cosy apocalypse
savoured
stood down

and hardly
not this time
the end of the world

To the M62

Grant me the slipstream of the lost,
the godspeed of all who have driven
east for Ireland and west for sunrise.
You will know your fellow travellers by
the backs of their heads and recognize
that face to face means only goodbye.
The hawk winging over the forecourt
flecks with a single drop of red
your diesel stain and its rainbow bleeds.
Watch in the truckstop's turning circle
the cabs' huge brows nod resignation
and slip right off, a brainpan of wires
earthed to a pair of tatty mudflaps.
A layby is a bed in air
hungry for your transient cargo
of sleep. I turn in eight feet up
and will not wake while the traffic lasts.
Find me beyond the service station
where the radio late shift drifts
to static. Take the space I have kept you:
arrive with me before dawn nowhere
but here, that is nowhere, and ours, alone.

Acknowledgements

Acknowledgements are due to the editors of the following magazines, periodicals and books where some of these poems, or versions of them, were published first: *Archipelago, Architexts* (Hull City Council, 2007), *Best Irish Poetry in English 2007/2008/2009/2010* (Munster Literature Centre), *Blast, Drift* (Hull City Council, 2008), *Fulcrum, The Guardian, Hide* (Hull City Council, 2010), *Identity Parade: New British & Irish Poets* (Bloodaxe, 2010), *The Irish Times, London Review of Books, Manchester Review, The Penguin Book of Irish Verse* (Penguin, 2010), *Oxford Poetry, Poetry Ireland Review, Poetry London, The Rialto, An Sionnach, Southword, TLS* and *Warwick Review.*

'Lament for Ali Farka Touré' was first published as a pamphlet by Rack Press (2008).

page 13 'the hobbling man' is a logo of the German beer, Schlenkerla (from *schlenkern*, to swing or to dangle).